Those Difficult Talks for PR Pros ™

How Best to Say
What Needs to Be Said
to Clients, Colleagues,
and Employees

Alan Cohen

With Foreword by Janet Tyler,

Co-CEO of Airfoil Public Relations

Alan Cohen

Praise for *Those Difficult Talks for PR Pros™*

"Tough feedback is a gift if prepared properly. Alan Cohen helps you with tips and examples to make challenging conversations productive and capable of invoking change."

Barri Rafferty, Senior Partner, Ketchum

"'I'm not very good at confrontation.' If that's your attitude, then the PR game isn't for you. In *Those Difficult Talks for PR Pros™*, Alan Cohen shows you why if managed correctly, confrontation can be your best friend. More importantly, he shows you why 90% of the time, the tough talks you so dread don't have to happen in the first place."

Peter Shankman, Founder, Help A Reporter Out (HARO)

"Alan Cohen's *Those Difficult Talks for PR Pros™* is a compelling work that should resonate at many levels with every public relations practitioner. Cohen adeptly leads us toward a practical resolution of a dilemma we constantly face, both in our professional and personal lives."

Johna Burke, Senior Vice President, BurrellesLuce

"As Michelin guides us through travel and food excellence, so does the great author and coach Alan Cohen guide public relations executives through the daily challenge of being our best. *Those Difficult Talks for PR Pros™* is a life preserver, not only for communications executives, but also for helping all of us to live a better life."

Keith Sherman, Keith Sherman & Associates Public Relations

"Not since *Fierce Conversations* has a book been so helpful in having those really difficult and conflict-ridden conversations. But this book is written specifically for PR professionals, those of us who know how to communicate, but have difficulty doing so when it comes to our own teams. Alan Cohen gives you the tools you need to never procrastinate the conversation you need to have today."

Gini Dietrich, CEO, Arment Dietrich

"Having tough talks is something most people would rather avoid at all costs. But being an effective leader means being courageous in both words and actions—especially when it involves others. Alan's approach gives PR leaders the strategy and the tools to engage those around us in intentional conversations with powerful results."

Elise S. Mitchell, President and CEO, Mitchell Communications Group, Inc.

3

"In a fraction of the time it takes to worry about how you are going to handle that conversation you have been dreading, you can read this smart and straightforward book and learn how to do it well. Alan Cohen provides a radical new way of approaching a challenge that comes up all too often in the public relations business. If you can't always have Alan at your side to coach you through high stakes conversations with clients, colleagues or friends, make sure this book is always within easy reach."
Merrill Rose, Principal, Option A Advisors, LLC

"No matter the management style, everyone can learn something from *Those Difficult Talks for PR Pros™*. From the misbehaving client to the out of line employee, Alan offers concrete steps that take the fear out of having the conversation and ultimately lead to a better result. I have seen his strategies completely change the tone of a conversation and lead people directly to the desired conclusion, on their own."
Jacqueline Kolek, Partner & Senior Director, Peppercom Strategic Communications

"*Those Difficult Talks for PR Pros™* is the quintessential resource for any public relations professional. Cohen masterfully explores the reasons why we shy away from engaging in tough talks with clients, employees and colleagues and provides the resources and tools for creating win-win situations through these conversations. The book is a must-have resource to be included on any industry leader's bookshelf."
Johanna Mouton, Executive Director, Pinnacle Worldwide, a leading organization of independently owned public relations firms

"Alan Cohen's experience as a former PR executive affords him a keen ability to understand the unique communications challenges that PR professionals face and provide them with pointed coaching. Alan taught junior staff at my agency how to actively listen and provide conversation points to clients and supervisors that yield positive results. He is the ideal choice for PR agencies who want to provide staff with effective communications training that they can immediately be put into action."
Aziza Johnson, Vice President, Kaplow Communications

Table of Contents

"When the going gets tough, the tough get going."

Alan Cohen

Foreword

My first encounter with Alan Cohen was a rescue mission. We were both attending a PRSA Counselors Academy conference in Las Vegas several years ago, but during the sessions my mind was focused on a very difficult talk that I knew I must have with one of our employees. The prospect of that conversation had been distracting me for days. I sought advice from Alan, who stayed up until 2:30 a.m. to help me prepare for the talk.

Alan hadn't even begun drafting this book at the time, but he already had developed a framework for difficult talks that provided me with the perfect guidance that I needed. Today, that employee continues to be a vital contributor to our agency and remains a good friend.

Alan's approach helped me separate my penchant for being a people pleaser—and the guilt that naturally accompanies that trait when relationship-threatening situations arise—from the content of the message I needed to deliver. I learned I can't just begin the talk by declaring, "You're wrong." I needed to create what Alan calls a win-win-win situation: a win for me, the employee and the agency. He helped me learn how to take the time to prepare and think about my own personal responsibility in the situation and not just focus on how to win an argument.

Too often, we PR pros become hung up in our own emotions when we engage in difficult talks. In my own instance, I was having flashbacks to another employee situation that did not turn out as well. Alan helped me discard my anxiety about past conversations to focus on my opportunities with future talks. He showed me that, when we must provide criticism, we can frame it so that it's constructive instead of confrontational.

We've all been the victims of difficult talks that ended badly— often because we valued being right more than resolving the situation in a positive way. Alan's process, as detailed in *Those Difficult Talks for PR Pros™*, demonstrates that the outcome should and can be an improved relationship among everyone involved. He

7

has made clear that, to win, we need to let go instead of holding tight.

Alan's understanding of public relations—as well as the mental and emotional makeup of PR people—positions him as a particularly valuable coach. Since that first meeting when he set my mind at ease, our agency has called on Alan frequently to provide guidance on managing the conversations between our senior staff and their team members. I feel that the techniques he has offered us are equally valuable in adjusting the way we should talk with clients, reporters and vendors, as well. In fact, I've used portions of his methodology in talking with my children and have had great success.

Alan's framework for preparing and conducting a difficult talk is very specific to communications professionals, and our own managers have been able to adopt his techniques very quickly. We've become so adept at using them that we don't even realize we are doing so; they've become gently ingrained in each of us.

I have found Alan's sense of humor and warmth to be very infectious, and I'm happy that he has channeled his personality through a book that can be shared across our profession.

Janet Tyler, APR

Co-CEO and Co-Founder

Airfoil Public Relations

Alan Cohen

1

Why Are Those Difficult Talks So Difficult For PR Pros?

Some people mistake weakness for tact. If they are silent when they ought to speak and so feign an agreement they do not feel, they call it being tactful. Cowardice would be a much better name.

Frank Medlicott, Member of Parliament, United Kingdom

Public relations professionals are some of the most extroverted people in the world. Ironically, they are also some of the most non-confrontational people on earth.

The craft of public relations is about finding, keeping and building healthy relationships between an organization (or individual) and key groups. PR people are fearless in talking to reporters, editors, community groups, analysts, activists, and all manner of stakeholders about the merits of the company, client, or cause they represent. But put them in a situation where they need to have a difficult conversation with a client, manager, or employee and many avoid the experience regardless of the cost. Some will even deceive themselves into thinking that the avoidance is really a virtue they call "diplomacy" or "tact."

In reality, these PR pros are hurting the relationships that matter most. But there is a better way. Here are strategies that can help PR professionals (in fact, anyone) constructively navigate the tough, but necessary, conversations.

Pop quiz: How would you answer these three questions?

1.   What if you could have difficult conversations easily, without delay, at almost the very moment an issue arises?

2.   What if you could handle personal confrontations in such a way that both you and the other party not only walked away with a plan of action to address the issue, but also with a deeper respect and admiration for one another?

3.   What would be the impact on your business performance (morale, accountability, retention, engagement) if you were able to be comfortable having those kinds of challenging conversations?

If any of these sound like questions you want the answers to, read on; this book is the key to improving the relationships that matter most.

No matter what your level of experience is with these types of difficult conversations, you can begin having dialogues that will accomplish all these goals and more. Regardless of your level of confidence, you can learn how to handle these conversations powerfully and gracefully. Truly, when done right, difficult talks will change your life for the better.

No doubt about it, tough talks require tact, which is a quality that a great Irish adage defines as "the ability to tell a person to go to hell in a way that makes him look forward to the trip."

No one is born with the tact essential to tackling life's needed difficult talks. Preparing for and engaging in them often requires that we first confront our beliefs about ourselves and those who impact our performance and well-being.

What Exactly Is a Difficult Talk?

Unclear about the essence of a difficult talk? Then imagine yourself in one of these scenarios:

Picture yourself as the head of a mid-sized business. One of your most important clients has a tendency to be verbally abusive toward individuals on your team. They literally shake every time he addresses them. His abusiveness has reached the point that no one wants to work on the account. So you need to address the client and make him aware of his behavior and its impact. But his is a huge, huge piece of business, and you fear that by candidly telling him what the situation is, you may lose the account.

Or, one of your best employees has been acting really erratically. Reports are coming back to you that this employee has changed, and you suspect it might be a substance-abuse issue. You need to bring up the concern, but you don't know how. What if you're wrong? What could that do to the relationship? But what if you're right and you fail to bring it up?

These are just two examples of difficult talks that can bring dread to even the most confident professional. The higher your position within your organization, the more often you'll be called upon to address these types of situations. When managers avoid confronting them, the challenges tend to fester and create even more negative energy. The avoidance may well send a message to the staff that bad behavior is tolerated. Ultimately this weak leadership doesn't serve anyone.

Conflict-Averse PR Pros

David C. Baker, the prominent consultant to PR agencies, suggests that the impulse to avoid difficult talks may be that the PR field tends to attract "non-confrontational, conflict-averse" individuals. They're often well-connected, well-liked people-pleasers who were disinclined to rock the boat in the past, he says, and so they lack the ability to engage in tough conversations. Consequently, "they keep clients and employees on too long, over-service clients, and under-price their agency's work."

Size also plays a role, in his opinion. Because, unlike other segments of the marketing communications industry, PR firms tend to be small, independent entities, whose principal is very deeply involved in the operation. Rather than delegate the task to someone more objective, the agency head is determined to satisfy the client by watering down pricing and value. (Again and again, the lowest quotes are given by the principal, who tends to be thinking of the next payroll and, because "we need the money," agrees to a low fee without considering how to make a profit.)

Could this describe you?

Top Ten of Those Difficult Talks PR Pros Report Having

In the fall of 2011, I asked 106 PR practitioners to identify what they considered to be the most difficult talks they'd ever experienced in their public relations careers. Each was invited to select three answers from a list of 25 possibilities (so the totals will not add up to 100%). Here's the top ten countdown.

10.   Asking for money owed you. 13.9%

9.   Telling a client that a story about his company or product was not going to be positive. 14.8%

8.   Confronting dishonest or unethical behavior. 17.8%

7.   Meeting with a colleague/employee who is not performing. 18.8%

6.   Discussing feelings of being taken advantage of or underappreciated by boss or employee. 19.4%

5.   Giving negative feedback to a manager or supervisor. 19.8%

4.   Telling the clients they cannot get what they want. 20.3%

3.   Pointing out that although an employee is working hard, they are not developing skills to advance to the next job level. 20.8%

2.   Breaking the news you're eliminating someone's job. 23.8%

1.   Addressing personality issues that are rubbing people the wrong way. 29.7%

A quick comment on the #1 difficult talk, which is people issues. My experience as a coach for public relations pros bears out this truism: the biggest problems people have are other people. In the words of a Dutch proverb: "The world is good, but the people could be a lot better."

The Toughest of the Tough

The toughest talks, according to one PR manager, always seem to center around promotions and money.

One extremely difficult conversation involved telling an employee she managed that he wasn't being promoted, even though she truly believed he was ready for advancement. But another manager, whose approval was needed, didn't agree.

The employee had fully expected to be given the promotion, so the turndown was quite a blow (to the point "there were tears and lots of them!"). Having to talk him through what was the other manager's opinion was hard, "especially because I completely disagreed with her and felt hopeless in the situation."

A more common reason for a difficult talk she needed to have with another employee she managed was "about his negative" energy and constant complaining about his account work, account load, and fellow team members.

"What made the chat especially tough was the fact he had many valid points," she says.

"He is overworked, overloaded and on a number of accounts that aren't aligned with his personal career growth path. He's also a top performing employee and one we want to keep here!"

As a result of the conversation, "he recognized the impact his negative energy was having on fellow employees and began making a concerted effort to take a step back before being so quick to complain."

This agency official credits coaching she'd received for teaching her how to have the conversation in a delicate way. As a result, it didn't come off as too rough but rather as a dialogue that was engaging and two-sided. "And in the end, my colleague didn't feel attacked, but felt he had a voice in the decision that we arrived at together."

The conversation also taught her some things about herself: "I can be harsh and too quick to judge, and often need to look at all the different viewpoints and weigh the different possible outcomes before making a decision. I also learned that people want to hear the truth—but there's a polite way to get your point across without coming off as abrasive."

Eight Reasons PR People Avoid Those Difficult Talks

In my Difficult Talks for PR Pros(SM) workshops, I've been gathering data on why people avoid tough talks.

First, let's make sure we are on the same page with our definition. A difficult talk is a potentially challenging and emotional conversation involving two or more people that addresses an important gap in, or dissatisfaction with, behavior, performance, or relationships. The goal should be clear communication, commitments, and a win-win solution. This can be difficult when you are confessing your own guilt or admitting a personal mistake.

Sounds great, but if difficult talks are so beneficial, why do so many people avoid having these exchanges? In my coaching, I've heard many reasons why people avoid difficult talks. These eight (in no particular order) come up over and over again:

"I lack the training to handle these types of conversations."

"It's out of my comfort zone."

"I feel afraid of what will happen."

"I feel vulnerable."

"I don't understand the other person."

"There are too many obstacles."

"It's too political."

"It takes too much time."

When these excuses are overcome, the benefits can be enormous. People feel more empowered. They discover they can make a difference. They develop closer, more collaborative relationships. Perhaps most important, people will respect that you have the courage to address a difficult situation.

Those Difficult Talks with Friends

It is bad enough when a difficult conversation is necessary with anyone. But, in some ways it's worse when the talk involves a friend.

The head of a PR agency had to tell a good friend—who was well-qualified for the job she was seeking—that she couldn't hire her because of her executive team's decision, which was partly due to their friendship.

"I explained that we had received numerous new resumes that were quite good and competitive with her qualifications. And that, in all fairness to us, we felt compelled to visit with some of these candidates. She understood this point."

Then, turning to the friendship issue, she told the candidate she'd received some feedback from the executive team that, while they liked the applicant, they were uncomfortable with her close friendship with the agency head.

"I shared my concerns about how tough it would be for her to overcome those concerns if she came on board. I also informed her that the firm's hiring process was collaborative and that if our team settled on another candidate either for qualifications or because of the friendship issue, we would go that route.

"This was harder for her to hear, but she said she could see why others might feel that way, although she felt her loyalty to me as a friend should be viewed as an asset in that we would be able to trust her to protect us financially on all points."

The difficult talk could have shattered their friendship.

But the agency head wrapped up the conversation "by stating how much I respected her as a professional and loved her as a friend. I asked her how she felt about the information I shared; then later asked how she felt about how I had handled the conversation. She was most grateful for honesty and openness and stated she trusted me to feel comfortable enough as a friend to have a tough talk with her."

While the candidate still wants the job, she said she would understand if the company didn't offer it to her. And how does the agency head feel about it?

"I'm glad I did it, and feel relieved and stronger for it."

Those Difficult Talks Are Habit, Not Native Skill

Before people can be the masters of difficult talks at home or in their professional life, they need to develop the habit of having them. They also need to give themselves an opportunity to find their own voice and approach, and put some proven tools into practice. No one is born with this ability; it must be learned along life's journey. Here are some principles to help guide you along the way.

An important point to ponder is this: the most difficult talk you will probably ever have is the one you're going to have with yourself about a number of different situations. Much of the process you are going to learn in this book has to do with self-reflection.

You need to really examine the facts of the situation in contrast with your beliefs about what's happening or is due to happen. In doing so, you're able to really show up for the difficult conversations with more integrity and thus stay true to yourself.

Old Joke File: Polite or Passive-Aggressive?

There is a common belief that some of the most tactful people on Earth are English. One office supervisor called a secretary in to give her the bad news that she was being fired. He started the conversation with: "Miss Symthe, I really don't know how we would ever get along without you, but, starting Monday, we're going to try."

Another English office manager told the staff, "You are the best employees in all of London that we could afford."

My Take on Those Difficult Talks

Every PR pro's concept of a difficult talk is different. But we often project onto situations our belief that a conversation is going to be difficult or challenging. As a result, we might avoid having it, when, in fact, it might not be a difficult conversation at all.

However, the negative energy that's being stockpiled by avoiding the conversation may result in a self-fulfilling prophecy, and may emerge in ways that aren't serving either the individual or the relationship well. Not confronting the situation has a price. Often avoidance just makes matters worse.

True confession time. Let me share what's drawn me to this topic, and some of what I see in my own consulting practice. It's been said that "we teach the things we need to learn." This topic has resonated for me a great deal over the past few years because I realized that I had a pattern of avoiding confrontation. I've seen this thread through my entire life: holding things in, keeping secrets, or not addressing situations head-on.

Much of this has to do with my people-pleasing nature, which in some ways pleases no one in the long run. Because when I don't express how I'm really feeling, it shows itself later in certain acting-out behavior.

Perhaps you can relate to this. I've reflected about some business relationships in which I no longer wanted to be involved.

But rather than confronting that issue head-on with my partner, I noticed myself engaging in unproductive behaviors, such as missing meetings, cutting back on the amount of work I performed, or showing a lack of enthusiasm for assignments. This is the kind of passive-aggressive behavior that makes a situation even worse. It's a kind of pattern that creates more pain than relief.

As I was looking for examples to illustrate this point, four different e-mails crossed my screen, each of which about a situation that I didn't want to deal with: financial discussions with people with whom I work, business relationship issues, somebody dropping the ball on a project, and personal matters.

Perhaps you can relate to some of those categories, or to the following five typical examples of concerns that have emerged in my coaching sessions with public relations firms and departments:

1.   HR managers having to take on all the difficult conversations with employees because the company's owners and senior executives don't want to engage in the tough talks.

2.   Newly promoted managers who don't know how to bring up difficult issues with friends who are now their subordinates.

3.   Peers avoiding having conversations with each other about performance.

4.   Employees telling their managers that they have lost trust in their peers.

5.   Vice presidents afraid to tell clients that what they want is unreasonable, unrealistic, or just plain wacky.

I've observed difficult talk avoidance across all roles and functions. Often, it's the more junior people feeling disempowered to ask their bosses directly for feedback. Plus it's the bosses feeling as though they don't have the time or energy to have one more conversation about performance. The same patterns and trends exist everywhere I go.

But in truth, sometimes a tough talk you were sure would go well turns out to be much the opposite, possibly because of unreasonable expectations.

For example, a PR specialist was going to hire away a valued employee of a PR department in which he formerly worked. As a courtesy and possibly out of subconscious guilt, he called the woman's current boss, a former colleague of his, hoping for her approval of the hiring. His expectation was way off the mark. Instead of being understanding of the plan, if not approving, the PR executive threatened to cut all ties, both business and personal, with him. She remained hostile for years.

Contributing to the severity of her reaction was his opening of the conversation with "You're not going to be happy with this…" That turned out to be a drastic understatement. At first, responding to her anger, he was almost ready to renege on his plan. But on reflection, he realized that doing that would be patently unfair to the hiree (who'd given notice) and to his own business. So he lived with the consequences of the difficult phone conversation that he'd felt he had to make.

The Goals of a Difficult Talk

To elaborate on a point made earlier about the goals of a tough talk, this is how I see it: to take responsibility for acting with personal integrity, to minimize behavior that undermines long-term success and happiness, and to maximize behavior that leads to long-term success and happiness.

In the PR business, difficult talks can take place between team members, an employer and an employee, a vendor and a client, a reporter and a publicist. In our personal lives they can take place between spouses, ex-spouses, whole families, friends, and partners. There are all sorts of permutations and combinations.

If you take away nothing else from this book, let it be this: difficult talks are essential to living a life of integrity, effectiveness, and true happiness. Difficult talks can make your relationships deeper and more rewarding than you can ever imagine. This is the main message of this book, and living it will change your life.

But What if I Just Left it Alone?

But, you may be thinking, won't it just work out? How many times have we all asked that? "Maybe if I just put my head in the sand about it, it's going to resolve itself." But that's generally not the case. Difficult talks take sacrifice and risk to overcome resistance and achieve desired results.

How much time have you spent wondering why the head of your company hasn't addressed an untenable situation or behavior? The problem is so obvious, you tell yourself, why is he or she avoiding being direct in communicating about it?

That communication failure diminishes the leader in your eyes, because he or she hasn't had the courage to step up and initiate the challenging conversation.

Naturally everyone is mindful of the formal authority structure and the fact that the persons above us can always take action against us if they don't like what they hear. So it's understandable

31

that we may be reluctant to step forward and have a conversation with them.

Obviously, it's natural to have some wariness about the people above us who have that power. That's why employees often make certain assumptions about what those in authority would do to them if they were told the truth. Yes, they have the power. But how much of our concerns are actually valid?

Concerned about their boss's reaction to frank conversation, staff members are often limiting their relationship, or in many ways impeding the leader's potential for successful management. And they threaten their own integrity and values by not having the conversation.

A person who places high value on honesty and fairness is choosing not to be honest and fair by avoiding the conversation. That decision knocks the employee out of alignment with his or her values, and that is an uncomfortable place to be.

Consider this: the pain of showing up every day at work feeling that disconnect is going to be much greater than the comfort from that paycheck. It's up to each of us to decide which path we want to take. Only you can decide what choices you want to make in those situations… choices with lasting consequences.

2

Why Those Difficult Talks Are Worth It

"A conversation is a dialogue, not a monologue," the author Truman Capote once said. "That's why there are so few good conversations: due to scarcity, two intelligent talkers seldom meet."

Ah, but if they do meet, the benefits can be tremendous.

Difficult talks bring significant rewards in moving us from fear to confidence. From separation to connection. From powerlessness to personal and social potency. And from low performance to exceptional, high performance.

There have been a host of recent studies about employee engagement. The findings are consistent about what, ultimately, people are really looking for from their leadership. The studies all indicate that while leaders are generally quite good at their business, they tend to lack the attributes their peers and employees highly regard: empathy, trustworthiness, and depth.

One role of leaders is to challenge the inequality and myths of command and control that exist in their companies. This is better than the leader attempting to socialize everyone into accepting the status quo.

Employees should be encouraged to talk to the person who is formally above them and address the tough issues that face the organization and their working relationship.

But know this also: difficult talks aren't about getting someone to do what it is that you want. Tough talks are really more about creating a synergistic relationship, exploring options, fostering engagement, and coming up with win-win solutions.

The organizations that prosper from this are those whose leaders realize that, for a difficult talk to be truly worthwhile, for it to be an honest give-and-take, status and position should be treated as irrelevant.

With organizations today flatter and less hierarchical, ideas and solutions, and the conversations that spawn them, are being initiated across all different levels.

Old Joke File: The Bachelor And His Cat

This is an old joke but it illustrates a point about talks needing to be handled with finesse. A bachelor who lived at home with his mother and pet cat went on a trip to Europe. Before he left he told his best friend to inform him of any emergencies.

A few days after his departure, his cat climbed up on the roof, fell off and was killed. His friend immediately texted him with the message: "Your cat died!"

The bachelor was back home the next day, having cut short his trip in grief and anger at his friend, whom he told "Why didn't you break the news to me gradually? You know how close I was to my cat! You could have sent a message, 'Your cat climbed up on the roof today,' and the next day you could have written, 'Your cat fell off the roof.' Then let me down slowly that he died."

After a quick memorial service, the bachelor left to continue his trip. A few days later as he was checking his e-mail at the hotel he saw a message from his friend. It read, "Your mother climbed up on the roof today."

Three Elements to Focus On

To benefit from difficult talks, there are three different areas to focus on: personal responsibility, resiliency, and emotional intelligence. Each area is like the leg of a three-legged stool that supports tough talks.

The first leg, personal responsibility, is about owning our part of the conversation. So rather than waiting for that other person to come speak to us, it's about taking the initiative. This helps people stay in alignment and true to their core beliefs, especially the beliefs about what is right and wrong.

The second leg, resiliency, is the capacity of people to cope with stress and adversity in a positive way. Both the giver and the receiver of a difficult talk need resiliency as a coping mechanism. This coping can manifest itself in the ability of both the person giving the tough talk and the one receiving it to "bounce back" after the discussion to a state of normal functioning. Being resilient also means having the difficult talk produce a "steeling effect," which helps the individual function better than expected in future tough talks. (The effect is much like an inoculation against a disease, in that it gives a person the capacity to cope well with future exposure.) Overall, to succeed, difficult talks take resiliency, not rigidity, from both parties.

The third leg, emotional intelligence, is your self-awareness. This means having empathy toward others, coupled with an ability to build healthy, rewarding relationships based on responsible decisions. So really, the essence of difficult talks involves showing up and taking personal responsibility for your own reactions, fears, judgments, and conclusions. You need to ask yourself whether your thoughts, emotions, judgments, or behaviors in this relationship are part of a pattern of how you consistently relate to others.

And, in order to respond, rather than react, it's important to let go of ego.

Vulnerability Is No Sin

Contrary to what many of us have been led to believe about how to act in the world of business, building successful relationships is about being open and, yes, even a little vulnerable. This vulnerability is much more about shedding our shells and personas, and letting others in, than it is about holding on to our shells and personas, and keeping others out.

For those of you who are familiar with the 12 steps of Alcoholics Anonymous and similar programs, the suggested approach involves taking personal responsibility and "keeping your side of the street clean." Before taking on a difficult talk, we all need to ask ourselves, "Where has my behavior possibly not brought out the best in the other person?"

It's important always to evaluate communication in terms of your behavior, your actions, and how you might not have presented yourself in the best way possible. It's also about the responsibility of just *having* the conversation, rather than hoping the issue is going to blow over or that the other person is going to be forthcoming.

Another important consideration is to release the outcome. This conversation is not about proving who is right and who is wrong. The need for better relationships is more important than the need to be right. When your objective is to prove that you are right, you can win the battle and lose the war. I've found that the real suffering comes when people become overly attached to what the outcome of the difficult talk is likely to be. Instead, be open to hearing what the other person has to say. Know that there probably will be some tricky twists and turns to navigate. In tough talks, it's imperative that you are resilient, and that you have faith you're going to get somewhere, without dwelling on the likely specific outcome of the conversation.

I find that even with colleagues, a difficult talk is symbolic of some theme or lesson I need to work on and eventually master. There's a reason I need to have this conversation. Typically, it's because there's something that I've avoided in my life and thus is a life lesson. I think of these talks as a chance to practice becoming a better person.

Chances are, if you don't have the difficult talk with this individual and process through it, the personality or behavior issue is going to recur again and again.

Every difficult talk is an opportunity to learn more about yourself, the other person, your own values and what's important to you. And to take more personal responsibility.

Sometimes in the process of doing the self-reflection, you may decide that it's not a conversation you *need* to have. But you may be choosing subconsciously to avoid having the conversation.

Perhaps in the grand scheme of things, the relationship is not that important to you. Or you feel that how you've handled it in the past is fine. Maybe you're choosing to handle it one more time, or not at all. Any of these decisions will emerge in self-reflection.

That's fine, because then the self-reflection will have helped you *consciously* choose to not have the conversation instead of that being the default choice. None of these is a case of avoiding a necessary talk because you're coming from a place of fear.

Often the fear comes from not knowing how to have the difficult talk. "I'm scared about what I may learn about the other person or myself," you might think. Or "I'm dismissing this person as unimportant." Any such fears would be more on an unconscious level. When it comes to having success with these talks, a goal might be to become more conscious in terms of your choices about whether or not to have conversations. When a person understands why he or she needs to have the conversation, such other questions as when and where to have the talk are easier to determine.

Old Joke File: The Sergeant and the Private

Difficult talks require reflecting before speaking. Here is another old joke to serve as a reminder to gather your thoughts before engaging in a tough talk.

The Captain called the Sergeant in. "Sarge, I just got a message from HQ that Private Jones' mother died yesterday. Better go tell him and send him in to see me." So the Sergeant calls for his morning formation and lines up all the troops.

"Listen up, men," says the Sergeant. "Johnson, report to the mess hall for KP. Garcia, report to Personnel to sign some papers. The rest of you men report to the Motor Pool for maintenance. Oh by the way, Jones, your mother died, report to the commander."

Later that day the Captain called the Sergeant into his office. "Hey, Sarge, that was a pretty cold way to inform Jones his mother died. Couldn't you be a bit more tactful, next time?"

"Yes, sir," answered the Sarge.

A few months later, the Captain called the Sergeant in again with, "Sarge, I just got a message from HQ that Private Wilson's wife died. You'd better go tell him and send him in to see me. This time be more tactful." So the Sergeant calls for his morning formation. "Ok, men, fall in and listen up. Every married man, take two steps forward. NOT SO FAST, WILSON!"

Principles to Consider

For many people, the reason these conversations are so difficult is because in the past they've had conversations that have blown up in their face.

Maybe it was because they didn't do much self-reflection before they had the difficult talk. Perhaps they didn't prepare or choose a time that would be optimal. Or they didn't look at things from the other person's perspective. That can result in less of a talk and more of a one-way hit-and-run. Most likely they didn't really care about what the other person had to say, or what the other person believed to be true about the situation. (A principle taught in Psychology 101: "What people believe is true for them and has social significance.")

There are many reasons why a tough talk may not have been as powerful and productive as it could have been. But people often make an assumption that every new (potentially confrontational) situation will go badly. They reason, "Oh no, he's just going to explode when I tell him that."

Well, yes, the person probably will explode if you approach the conversation the same way as you did the last time, and the time before that and the time before that.

What I'm advocating in this book is actually a different way to approach these conversations.

The first principle to consider is that engaging in difficult talks is just a habit, not a talent. Difficult talks are like being a great painter. You learn a process. You're schooled in how to paint. And then ultimately you throw that away because painting has become a part of your DNA. Engaging in successful difficult talks is more about internalizing the principles that are going to guide the conversations than learning the steps.

Look at everyone as a growth stock. What you invest in a person in conversations is going to reap significant benefits to you in your life. These talks will also profit them, if you are respectful to the other person and to the importance of having the conversation. On the other hand, sometimes the result of a difficult talk is that the relationship ends. This is not always a bad outcome. Sometimes the better path for both parties is to go their separate ways.

Each person is a teacher and a student. So we learn as much from the person we're having a conversation with, as they ideally are going to be learning from us. Mutual respect and mutual purpose is the foundation of success. So you should always be thinking about not only what's best for *you*, but also what's best for the other person and what's best for the relationship.

Think not only about difficult talks in terms of the outcome of this conversation, but from within a more spiritual context. What's best for this person? What's potentially best for this relationship over time?

Individuals' behavior is not who they are, but merely reflects certain choices they've made or are making. No one is this or that. People just behave in this way or that way.

When we enter into a difficult talk, we need to be keenly aware of how we're labeling or generalizing the behavior of others, and the language we use to refer to the behavior. For example, take this phrase: "You're toxic, and I barely want anything to do with you."

Terrible, right? What feelings would you have if someone said that to you? "You're toxic." How would that impact on how you relate to the speaker?

No doubt the reaction would be different if the message were delivered in the following manner: "Your behavior has been very challenging for me to work with. I often feel close to the point of giving up. I would very much appreciate it if we could sit down privately and talk openly about this."

How would that make you feel if someone said that to you? Certainly better than if he or she labeled you as toxic. The lesson is: don't express a judgment of the person with whom you're having the difficult talk. Instead, express difficulty or disappointment with the behavior. There's a world of difference when you take this approach. (The renowned child psychologist, Haim Ginott, used to advise that if your child accidentally were to spill a glass of milk, you should not attack his personality, exclaiming, "You're a klutz, you always were a klutz, you always will be a klutz!" Instead, empathize with him over the fact an unfortunate mishap had taken place, and "let's clean it up together.")

Every person is so much more interesting and complex than any of us give credit for in the business world. And, by the way, these principles apply equally to your relationships with family, friends, and partners. People should not be one kind of person at work and another kind of person at home. Engaging in difficult talks is about showing up with integrity in all your relationships.

3

Difficult Talks Self-Assessment

The Canadian writer Margaret Millar was noted for saying that "most conversations are simply monologues delivered in the presence of a witness." Unfortunately, that is the mindset of many who decide they need to have a tough talk with someone.

My definition of a difficult talk, however, is a conversation that truly involves two or more people addressing an important gap in behavior or performance and ends with a clear commitment to a solution that, if not a win for both sides, at least provides something both sides can live with.

When do you need to have a difficult talk? When the current situation of behavior pattern disturbs your peace and your ability to perform at optimum levels. Here are five sure signs.

1.   If, in thinking about this relationship, you feel a negative charge inside yourself, then your peace is disturbed.

2.   If you are going about your day and, seemingly out of the blue, you think about this relationship and feel yourself tighten up, then your peace is disturbed.

3.   If you think about this person and your energy level goes down instead of up, then your peace is disturbed.

4.   If you actively avoid this person, so as not to have to deal with the issue, then your peace is disturbed.

5.   If you are acting out on issues in any way, instead of dealing openly with them, then your peace is disturbed.

Whenever any of that happens, it's time to consider having a difficult talk. But are you willing to engage candidly in these talks? As Socrates put it, often the key to life is to "know thyself." To assess your views about having difficult talks, ask yourself if you agree or

disagree with the following personal statements:

Question	Agree	Disagree
I occasionally have a hard time communicating to people that what I want them to do is in their best interests.		
I sometimes find myself getting angry too easily.		
I sometimes blame problems on others and later find I was partially to blame.		
I sometimes talk myself out of discussing problem behavior because I don't want a difficult confrontation.		
I have a tendency to "book people on guilt trips" or make threats to get them to do what I want.		

I tend to put off discussions longer than I should, to avoid getting into an argument.		
When I confront people, I sometimes talk only about the easy problem, not the big, root problem.		
I would have a better life if I could find a way to have honest conversations without taking too much risk.		
I tend not to be able to motivate people to do what I want because I lack the power to force them to do it.		
I tend to bring up the same issues over and over again.		
I sometimes find it difficult to give people honest feedback without offending them.		

I often assume that the people who are causing me problems are doing it on purpose.		
I have people I deal with who just can't seem to get motivated.		
I sometimes give people assignments but lack the time and energy to follow up to see if they accomplished the tasks.		
When I assign people a task they don't like, I put pressure on them so they will have to complete the job.		
I tend to believe that people at my work and home think that I micromanage them.		

I sometimes get sidetracked in a conversation about an issue and forget the original problem.		
I sometimes forget to give clear deadlines and then am disappointed when my expectations are not met.		
When people get angry during a discussion, I often don't know how to respond.		
When someone misses a deadline or commitment, I sometimes let it slide.		
I sometimes forget to check up on people who committed to do something.		
I sometimes ask people for their ideas and opinions, although I don't really want them because I already have a solution.		

I sometimes make it hard for others to bring up their views during a problem-solving discussion.		
I sometimes talk too much and listen very little when I discuss a problem with others.		
I often will make sure we talk about my issues during a discussion, but leave little time for others to talk about theirs.		

How to Score Your Self-Assessment

21-25 agrees	There is much to work on
15-19 agrees	There are many principles yet to learn
6-14 agrees	There are some strategies and tactics yet to learn
1-5 agrees	You should teach others about Those Difficult Talks

An Important Thought About Scoring

No matter what your numerical score on this assessment, please know this: your numerical score is not who you are.

You are not somehow better or superior because the assessment indicates you are a masterful tough-talker; nor are you lesser or inferior because the assessment indicates you really need to work on developing your skills. What you are, and what everyone is, is simply a human being in a process of learning. Each of us has vast untapped resources of skill, potential, and value. This assessment is just information.

Old Joke File: Cracking the Performance Evaluation Code

Speaking of assessments, think of all those difficult talks that are avoided during performance reviews (or the lack of performance reviews). I am not sure where this old joke originated, but it is a winner (I found it on http://www.careerdfw.org).

Some of you might like to know what the supervisor is really saying in all those glowing employee work performance evaluations that are cranked out.

AVERAGE: Not too bright.

EXCEPTIONALLY WELL QUALIFIED: Has committed no major blunders to date.

ACTIVE SOCIALLY: Drinks heavily.

ZEALOUS ATTITUDE: Opinionated.

CHARACTER ABOVE REPROACH: Still one step ahead of the law.

UNLIMITED POTENTIAL: Will stick with us until retirement.

QUICK-THINKING: Offers plausible excuses for errors.

TAKES PRIDE IN WORK: Conceited.

TAKES ADVANTAGE OF EVERY OPPORTUNITY TO PROGRESS: Buys drinks for superiors.

INDIFFERENT TO INSTRUCTION: Knows more than superiors.

STERN DISCIPLINARIAN: A real jerk.

TACTFUL IN DEALING WITH SUPERIORS: Knows when to keep mouth shut.

APPROACHES DIFFICULT PROBLEMS WITH LOGIC: Finds

someone else to do the job.

A KEEN ANALYST: Thoroughly confused.

NOT A DESK PERSON: Did not go to college.

EXPRESSES SELF WELL: Can string two sentences together.

SPENDS EXTRA HOURS ON THE JOB: Miserable home life.

CONSCIENTIOUS AND CAREFUL: Scared.

METICULOUS IN ATTENTION TO DETAIL: A nitpicker.

DEMONSTRATES QUALITIES OF LEADERSHIP: Has a loud voice.

JUDGMENT IS USUALLY SOUND: Lucky.

MAINTAINS PROFESSIONAL ATTITUDE: A snob.

KEEN SENSE OF HUMOR: Knows lots of dirty jokes.

STRONG ADHERENCE TO PRINCIPLES: Stubborn.

GETS ALONG EXTREMELY WELL WITH SUPERIORS AND SUBORDINATES ALIKE: A coward.

SLIGHTLY BELOW AVERAGE: Stupid.

OF GREAT VALUE TO THE ORGANIZATION: Turns in work on time.

UNUSUALLY LOYAL: Wanted by no-one else.

ALERT TO COMPANY DEVELOPMENTS: An office gossip.

REQUIRES WORK-VALUE ATTITUDINAL READJUSTMENT: Lazy and hard-headed.

HARD WORKER: Usually does it the hard way.

ENJOYS JOB: Needs more to do.

HAPPY: Paid too much.

WELL- ORGANIZED: Does too much busywork.

COMPETENT: Is still able to get work done if supervisor helps.

CONSULTS WITH SUPERVISOR OFTEN: Annoying.

WILL GO FAR: Relative of management.

SHOULD GO FAR: Please.

USES TIME EFFECTIVELY: Clock-watcher.

VERY CREATIVE: Finds 22 reasons to do anything except original work.

USES RESOURCES WELL: Delegates everything.

DESERVES PROMOTION: Create new title to make them feel appreciated.

4

Preparing For Those Difficult Talks: The Checklist

In my opinion, one of the most important books in recent years for public relations or, for that matter, any other profession, is *The Checklist Manifesto* by Atul Gawande. "We have an opportunity before us, not just in medicine but in virtually any line of work," writes Gawande. "Even the most expert among us can gain from searching out the patterns of mistakes and failures and putting a few checks in place."

Avoidable failures are common and persistent, not to mention demoralizing and frustrating, across many fields—from medicine to finance, air travel to government. According to Gawande, the reason is increasingly evident: the volume and complexity of what we know has exceeded our individual ability to deliver its benefits correctly, safely, or reliably. Knowledge has both saved us and burdened us.

In all of his work as a surgeon and author, Gawande has devoted himself to learning how to improve the practice of medicine, a high-risk enterprise fraught with danger, uncertainty, and ever-growing complexity, where errors are matters of life and death. When asked by the World Health Organization to lead a global project to find ways to reduce deaths and complications in surgery, Gawande turned his attention to how people cope with risk and complexity in a variety of fields, from skyscraper construction to aviation to venture capital.

Surprisingly, he found the most successful approach not in greater technology or more training but in the humblest of tools: the checklist. And when he and his team applied a checklist to surgery, the results were dramatic: death rates and complications fell by more than a third. Less than a year after the release of these stunning results, 20 countries and thousands of hospitals are committed to adopting the WHO surgery checklist. In the checklist, Gawande found a mighty idea that has the potential to transform medicine and many other fields whose complexity has outstripped the ability of an individual to get things right.

Think of a situation you are currently experiencing that could benefit from a difficult talk. In particular, describe the gap between what you observe is happening and what you desire to be happening. Here is a checklist to help you prepare.

Your Those Difficult Talks Prep Checklist

Step 1

HOW ARE YOU EXPERIENCING THIS SITUATION?

What emotions do you experience about this situation?

What beliefs do you hold about it?

What judgments have you made about the person/people involved?

How have you and the people with whom you interact altered your/their behavior as a result of this situation?

Step 2

WHAT ARE YOUR CORE VALUES IN LIFE?

How has the current situation violated or threatened your values?

Examine the behavior of the other(s) as well as your own.

Articulate clearly what values you truly want to stand for.

Step 3

WHAT OPPORTUNITIES ARE BEING PRESENTED BY THIS SITUATION?

How could you use this situation to honor your values and have a positive impact on society and your own self-esteem?

Step 4

WHERE CAN YOU TAKE GREATER PERSONAL RESPONSIBILITY?

How have you projected your own reactions onto the situation itself— and blamed the circumstances or the people involved for them?

REMEMBER: No one other than you is responsible for your emotions, beliefs, judgments, and behaviors. Between any stimulus and your response is a space in which you choose how you react.

Any person or situation may influence your response, but you are the producer of your response; ultimate responsibility for your choices is therefore yours.

When you rise above patterns of justifying, rationalizing, self-victimizing, and hyper-sensitivity in order to take personal responsibility, you become an agent of change.

Step 5

WHAT ARE YOUR NEW AWARENESSES?

How have your perceptions of the situation and yourself shifted as a result of taking these first four steps?

What's the deeper learning opportunity this situation seems to be presenting you?

Connect inside and appreciate your having released upset emotions, beliefs, and judgments.

Step 6

WHAT ARE THE FACTS AND ISSUES BEING PRESENTED IN THIS SITUATION?

Get curious about these! Often we make assumptions based on a very limited or incorrect set of facts and issues. If we can pull back to examine the entire situation—instead of making negative judgments about the other person's disposition—the complete facts and correct issues will often become perfectly clear.

FACTS: What is actually happening in the situation (to yourself, others, circumstances)?

ISSUES: What are the reasons you believe these things are happening (to yourself, others, circumstances)?

Step 7

WHAT ARE SOME POSSIBLE COURAGEOUS SOLUTIONS?

Based on your core values and what you believe are the facts and issues, what new strategies (thoughts and behaviors) could you adopt to become part of a positive solution to this situation?

In this step, refrain from editing yourself and over-thinking. Tap into your creative mind and list as many possibilities as you can imagine.

To see solutions from different perspectives, you can ask yourself imaginative questions such as: What would be the smallest solution? The boldest? The easiest? The most radical? The most unexpected? The most obvious? The most honest? The most courageous? The most caring? The one you'd suggest if you believed anything was possible?

Step 8

OF THESE, WHICH COULD MAKE THIS SITUATION A WIN-WIN-WIN?

What solutions could be a win for you? Now, set aside your own perspective and step into the other person's shoes to see the situation from that individual's point of view. Connect empathetically and imagine his or her thoughts, emotions, relationships, and responsibilities in this situation.

What solutions could be a win for the other person? Finally, what solutions could be a win for the relationship? (Solutions for the relationship support long-term positive outcomes that transcend the specific situation that you are addressing.)

Consider also what training, mentorship, and support (on both sides) may be instrumental for providing ongoing encouragement for a winning outcome.

Visualize success.

Step 9

WHEN WILL YOU INITIATE THIS CONVERSATION?

What's your next step for scheduling your tough talk?

What's your optimum timeline?

Example: A Completed Checklist

Situation:

My business partner frequently becomes unhinged and begins speaking at me with such hostility that I often feel like standing up in the middle of one of her diatribes and saying to her, "I quit. I don't deserve this. You deal with it." I've begun to dread coming to work in the morning, and once I'm there, can't wait for the day to be over so I can get away from her. I realize this is truly impacting my performance, and I've stopped making an effort to contribute new ideas or discuss the one's she puts forth. I just do whatever she says. I don't care. And I don't want to live nine hours a day feeling like this—so small and hopeless.

Step 1: HOW ARE YOU EXPERIENCING THIS SITUATION?

My relationship with my partner has made me feel so angry inside. Sometimes I flush hot and feel like I hate her—even when I'm not at work. Yet when I go into the office, I actually feel scared of her. I always wonder what mood she'll be in that day. And then I get so judgmental of myself and call myself a coward for not speaking up and for playing small. I've realized that in my personal life I've felt less boisterous than I used to be and it's like I just want to go home and hibernate after work. It's affecting my romantic relationship as well. Who wants to spend so much time with someone always in a funk and feeling hopeless? At the same time, I like what the company does and see so much potential here.

Step 2: WHAT ARE YOUR CORE VALUES IN LIFE?

What drew me to the company was its vision of empowered young professionals choosing to use their abilities to make a positive difference in the world—to speak out for important social issues, to collaborate to bring awareness to social injustice, to put their energies into building careers that fulfill them and inspire others rather than into self-destructive choices. Wow, it's true that one of my greatest values is speaking out for injustice so that we can collaborate in respect to build a more humane society. So interesting how I haven't been doing that in my relationship with my partner. Another value of mine is kindness towards others because I never know what they've been through and are trying to deal with. I haven't been being particularly compassionate toward my partner. It's been months since I had a kind thought toward her. No wonder I've been feeling so small and lost and upset; I haven't been honoring core values.

Step 3: WHAT OPPORTUNITIES ARE BEING PRESENTED IN THIS SITUATION?

My relationship with her is giving me a crucial opportunity to come back to honoring my core values and embrace the reasons that drew me to this company to begin with! I'm not sure yet how I'm going to actually address this, but I do see that the essence of the conflict is not how she has behaved, but how I have reacted to it and not stood for the values I hold that are most important to me. No matter how she has behaved, I can respond from my values. There is no rule in life that says staying true won't take effort! This is really an opportunity for me to build my resiliency and make much stronger choices in my life.

Step 4: WHERE CAN YOU TAKE GREATER PERSONAL RESPONSIBILITY?

I have judged her as wrong, unconscious, manipulative, and toxic. I realize that all of my judgments are projections of my own, based on the stories I am choosing to tell myself about my experience, and that she is not any of those things. She is a human being in a world in which she is doing the best she knows how to do to live successfully. Her behavior can either upset me or not—it is my choice. I choose to see it as a teacher that is currently giving me many opportunities to take responsibility for my own judgments and then come forward actively and kindly standing up for my values. If I successfully do this and decide that a kinder, healthier relationship has not developed, I can always leave. Not because I judge her as wrong, but rather, because I choose to stand up for my values and work in environments where there are others who choose behaviors based on the same set of values. Wow, my partner is actually giving me an opportunity to become much stronger and more vocal in standing up for who I am—actually what I want to support others in doing!

Step 5: WHAT ARE YOUR NEW AWARENESSES?

I feel so much different about going into work tomorrow now. I feel lighter. I feel like my entire perspective has changed. I feel more ready to address the dynamic in our relationship that I have been responding to so reactively these last few months. I feel like life has truly presented me with a test of character. Who said I was supposed to get along fabulously with all the people who I will ever work with? Sometimes it takes outrage to stand up and say, "The status quo is not working for me. I want to transform this situation so we can both be more effective and see new possibilities for working together." I feel like I like myself again. I know who I am and trust in the value and integrity of that.

Step 6: WHAT ARE THE FACTS AND ISSUES PRESENTED IN THIS SITUATION?

Well, the facts are that the company isn't performing as well as she had hoped. Because of how young the company is, other businesses are reluctant to partner with us. It's also unexpectedly become a saturated market. I know my partner is struggling with how to truly differentiate the company from its closest competitors and winning the respect of the local community. In the last six months, we've only begun two new partnerships of the six we pursued, and I haven't been involved in this process when I know she wanted me to be. The issues are that I haven't been involved because she wants to control all the communication and correspondence between the potential partners and us, so I don't really know what's going on to even begin to help. Yeah, the major issue seems to be one of control, trust, and fear. Ah, it's not really that she's just manipulative and toxic, she's afraid. She hasn't run a company before. This makes sense! We have to deal with the fear directly and learn how to trust each other—then we can truly bring all our creativity to making this company a success.

Step 7: WHAT COULD BE SOME COURAGEOUS SOLUTIONS?

Hmm... I wonder what would happen if, next time, when she slams the phone down and angrily calls me in from her office, I walk in, and acknowledged that in her voice I really could hear her anger, and have compassion for her experience. In fact, I wonder what might happen if I began a conversation with her by acknowledging how much of herself I see that she invests in the company and that I can't imagine the stress she must sometimes feel when her pitches to potential partners don't yield the results she wanted. I want to share this with her and let her know that I truly want to help her succeed—and at the same time let her know that when she takes her stress out in our relationship it makes it very hard for me to feel safe in her corner, and as committed as I want to be to the company's success.

Another idea is to set up a daily meeting with her in the morning and briefly discuss what is happening, what the underlying challenges and how we can best collaborate on achieving success in addressing them. This would give me an opportunity first thing in the morning to practice speaking up, show her that I'm committed to this company and engaged enough that she can trust me, and also treat her with kindness and compassion—especially that part of her that is understandably afraid of doing the wrong thing.

Step 8: OF THESE, WHICH COULD MAKE THIS SITUATION A WIN-WIN-WIN?

I think what would make it a win-win situation for me is if I could begin to speak up for my values and my ideas freely and experience a heartfelt, trusting, and collaborative relationship with my partner.

I think for her she really wants me to contribute my creative ideas and not just do what she says—she wants the person she started this business with! She also wants to know that she can trust me to follow through. I haven't been doing that lately. I'm ready to get back to that!

I think for the relationship a win would be if we could begin discussing how to more clearly define our roles. This would create a clear framework for how we move forward.

Step 9: WHEN WILL YOU INITIATE THE CONVERSATION?

Tomorrow morning I am going to ask her as early as possible for 15 minutes where I can bring up my concerns, my intentions and desires, and ask her to schedule a longer period of time later in the week for us to sit down and truly discuss how we can improve our working relationship.

Be Calm Before the Storm

Ideally, unpleasant situations should be dealt with as soon as possible, but David C. Baker, a PR consultant quoted in an earlier chapter issues a caveat: don't deal with a problem until you've calmed down and thought out the entire scenario.

Talk with somebody else about it first, he suggests. Someone who can help you see where and how your emotions might be getting in the way.

And he makes a great point: "Recognize that most of the time when a client and an employee complain about something, it's very seldom really about the complaint itself; there is something else behind it…and it is almost always personal."

He further points out, the tension you feel more often comes from what you don't talk about than from what you do talk about. So it is imperative, once you're calm, to deal with the issue as soon as possible.

Baker likes to prepare the person for whom the tough talk is intended by sending an e-mail, along the lines of "I think it's probably time that we explore this issue further, and I wonder if I could meet you tomorrow at such and such time." That gets the person in the right mood emotionally, so it doesn't come as a complete surprise, and he or she is much more likely to handle it well.

Quick Tip: Tactful Ways to Say "You're Wrong"

No one's right all of the time. When it's your job to set the record straight, flat-out telling someone he or she is wrong isn't the best way to get your point across. Why? It will make the person defensive and put an end to effective communication. Instead, say:

1. "I see your point, and I think…"
If you say, "but I…" you're saying you really don't see the person's point. Using the word "and" makes the individual feel that he or she has a good point, just not one that's valid right now.

2. "Hmmmm, what if we…"
This proves you've been listening and have considered the person's thoughts, and have an idea that'll work for both of you.

3. "The way I see it…"
This phrase suggests that you have a different opinion—not that the other person's opinion is wrong.

Adapted from *What's Working in Human Resources*, April 22, 2011

5

Having The Difficult Talk: The Checklist

Food for thought as you prepare for your next difficult talk: in the 1950 Japanese crime drama *Rashomon*, a rape and murder in a forest are reported by three witnesses, each from his or her own point of view. The witnesses tell a similarly structured story—that a man kidnapped and bound a samurai so that he could rape the wife—but each account ultimately contradicts the others. The witnesses are a notorious bandit who allegedly murdered the samurai and raped his wife; the white veil-cloaked wife of the samurai; and the samurai himself, who testifies through the use of a medium.

Who is telling the truth? What is truth?

As I watched the movie, I thought about some of my own experiences in corporate coaching, where members of a team individually recount their version of a story, and each version contradicts that of another team member. For each team member, his version was the only true version of what happened. How could that be? How could each version of the same event differ so dramatically?

I thought about how, in my own life, my interpretations of situations are not always accurate either. Often, in looking at a situation, I choose a less-empowering "story" for why things have happened.

When we believe that our perception of a situation is the only right one, and fail to see other perspectives and the interrelationship or connectedness of other factors (i.e. tunnel vision), we may be limiting our potential and possibilities. Remember, we each see things through our own unique DNA, our own lens, our own experience, values, culture, and beliefs.

Interpretations are opinions and judgments that we create about an event, situation, person, or experience. Our interpretation is what we believe is true. Maybe we're right, but maybe there are many other ways to see it.

The same can be true with a situation that requires a difficult talk. How might your interpretation of a situation of a circumstance be limiting you? Are you stuck in the box of your own account for what is occurring?

Having a tough talk can seem complex at first. So follow these guidelines to improve your outcomes.

Your Those Difficult Talks Checklist

Step 1

SHARE THE FACTS AND ISSUES AS YOU UNDERSTAND THEM

Start with: "I asked to meet with you today because I wanted to discuss…"

Describe the situation that you have initiated this tough talk to address.

In particular, describe the gap between what you observe to be happening and what you *want* to be happening.

Share with clarity, brevity, and a desire to fully communicate the circumstances from your point of view.

Step 2

SHARE HOW THIS SITUATION HAS AFFECTED YOU

Next tell them: "This is affecting me in the following manner..."

Because you will have already taken responsibility, you will be able to share this information from a place of insight, caring, and equanimity—humanizing both yourself and the other person—instead of from a place of emotional charge and victimization.

Step 3

SHARE YOUR VALUES

What are the core values you identified in the checklist in Chapter 4?

How has this situation challenged them?

What do you value about your relationship with this person?

Affirm from a sincere place *who* you see them to truly be, *how* they are valuable to you, and *why* they are worth this talk.

This is your opportunity to affirm mutual respect, mutual purpose, and create a safe environment for what could quickly be perceived as a threatening conversation.

Reaffirm these values throughout the tough talk.

Step 4

INVITE THEIR CANDID AND HONEST RESPONSE

Here is when you say: "I'm very interested in hearing your perspective on this. I am committed to doing my best to work together with you to identify a solution that will be a win for both of us."

Stay curious! Ask questions to verify that your understanding of the situation is accurate. Listen for the underlying issues and concerns that may not be being expressed.

Compliment the other(s) for being willing to share their perspective with you.

REMEMBER: No one other than you is responsible for your emotions, beliefs, judgments, and behaviors.

Take personal responsibility for any of your reactions that you become aware of while listening to the other person's perspective.

Look for the opportunities these present to return to your core values, learn, and become an agent of greater change.

Step 5

DISCUSS THE SITUATION TO REACH UNDERSTANDING AND AGREEMENT

This requires give and take.

Step 6

WHAT COULD BE SOME COURAGEOUS SOLUTIONS BASED ON THIS?

Invite and welcome the creativity and collaboration of others!

Be ready and willing to contribute the solutions that you already envisioned, if they still apply.

Collaborate in the discovery process by posing some of the imaginative questions that you may have used in Chapter 4.

If the other party or parties involved in the discussion request additional time to articulate solutions, honor the request.

Schedule a time in the near future to pick up the conversation and keep the commitment.

Step 7

OF THESE, WHICH COULD MAKE THIS SITUATION A WIN-WIN-WIN?

Go for the gold: a win for them, a win for you, and a win for the relationship.

Consider also what training, mentorship, and support (on both sides) may be instrumental in providing the ongoing encouragement for a winning outcome.

Take time to visualize success as a team and clarify whether the solutions devised will be the most effective for achieving your goals.

Step 8

WHICH SOLUTION ARE YOU CHOOSING?

What are the specific next steps?

Who is accountable for what?

By when?

Step 9

KEEP YOUR INTEGRITY. FOLLOW UP.

Follow through and follow up. Positive effort, worthwhile risk, and behavioral change all thrive in conditions of trust and integrity.

By following through and following up, you demonstrate that the issues, the person, and the relationship are in fact important to you.

Quick Tip: Delivering Bad News at Work

Career expert and best-selling writer Nicole Williams is the author of *Wildly Sophisticated: A Bold New Attitude for Career Success* (2004) and *Earn What You're Worth* (2005), published by Penguin Group Inc. Her latest *book, Girl on Top*, was published in 2009 by Hachette Book Group.

Williams writes: "Sometimes delivering bad news is unavoidable. But if you're stuck being the messenger, ensure that you get your point across as painlessly (and diplomatically) as possible. We asked personal development coach Julie Clements of Faith Performance, a coaching firm in the UK, for some tactful tips."

Situation #1: Your co-worker is a noisy, gossipy, unprofessional distraction.

What You Want to Say: "Be quiet! I'm trying to work here."

What You Should Say: "I love hanging out with you outside of the office, but during work hours, I get easily distracted. I'm considering moving desks. Is that cool with you?"

Why It Works: "You're praising her personality and giving her the power back by asking for her input," says Clements. "Just make sure you tell her this when you're alone. You don't want to call her out in front of the entire staff."

Situation #2: You have to fire an employee—one who's been a thorn in your side since he got there.

What You Want to Say: "I've been dreaming about the day I'd finally be rid of you."

What You Should Say: "Your contributions have been valued, but you're just not the right fit for our company and we're letting you go. Would you like to collect your things or have them sent to you?"

Why It Works: The "positive–negative–positive" pattern is very powerful, says Clements. Keeping your tone the same throughout helps the positive comments ease the way to and from the crunch moment.

Adapted from http://www.divinecaroline.com.

6

Top Ten Difficult Talks Troubles

Even though I subscribe to the idea that there are NO MISTAKES (mistakes are just things we label after the fact when they don't go as anticipated), there are some troubles you should avoid.

I say let's not label them "mistakes" if we can learn from them. There are errors, such as in arithmetic, spelling, etc., but in general we are doing the best we can in the moment. No one I know ever *chooses*, in the moment, to make a "mistake."

So here are those things that we traditionally might label mistakes. Instead, let's call them the top ten difficult talk troubles:

1. **Not preparing for a difficult talk**. Just winging it is never a good idea. These conversations can be slippery slopes if you are not prepared.

2.   **Not considering the head space that the other person might be in**. A confused, depressed or exhausted mind will not be receptive to having a tough talk.

3.   **Having the talk in front of other people**. Who likes to look bad in front of others? PR life can be hectic, but that is not an excuse for pointing out flaws in front of others.

4.   **Doing it when we are in a fraught emotional state**. Consider your emotions, too. When you're stressed, you can easily say something you wish you hadn't.

5.   **Bringing in lots of examples.** Forget the "if one is good, a dozen would be better" school of thought. Bombarding the person with a long list of sins is essentially "throwing the kitchen sink" at the other person. One or two examples will suffice.

6. **Not being willing to listen to the other person.** A difficult talk isn't a monologue in which you get to tell another person, "You know what your problem is?" This should be a two-way street.

7. **Focusing more on winning the fight than thinking about the long term of the relationship.** You can win the battle and lose the war. The real prize is an improved relationship.

8. **Being too attached to being right.** New facts and viewpoints often arise during a tough talk. Proving that "I'm right and you are wrong" is counter-productive.

9. **Having the talk when either party is too tired, too hungry or too irritable.** There is a right time and a wrong time for everything. PR pros lead hectic lives and sometimes choose the expedient course.

10. **Procrastinating about having the tough talk until a situation explodes**. The great hope is that the problem will work

itself out. This is the great false hope. Choose the right time, but don't keep putting it off.

The Benefits of Not Taking Shortcuts

Investing the time in doing tough talks right can pay dividends. Here is an example from a client of mine, a senior account executive from a mid-sized PR agency, who was finding that one of her employees was not meeting deadlines in creating an editorial calendar that she had requested numerous times. She was finding herself becoming incredibly irritated. I asked her to use the "Those Difficult Talks" approach, and let me know how it went.

"I wanted to circle back with you to let you know that the tough talk went better than expected," the client recently wrote to me. "I took the approach of 'how can I help you?' And, from what I discovered, she suffers from a similar issue that I have. She wanted to have this editorial calendar perfect the very first time around, and it was paralyzing her from getting started. Even after the suggestions we presented, she was analyzing the project all the way down to the appropriate format it should be in."

My client did not make the misstep of taking a "my way or the highway" approach. Instead, she invested time in understanding the viewpoint of her employee. The conversation was not about proving who was right.

"We took time to discuss how I am very confident in the work that she produces and like the ideas that she brings to the table. And I told her to imagine what she would want to see on an editorial calendar, and this should help her develop it without issue.

"Sure enough, I had the editorial calendar one hour later."

Quick Tip: Give Negative Feedback Positively
By Helen Jane Hearn, as told to American Express Open Forum

Giving people negative feedback is tricky. You don't want to hurt feelings or come across too harshly, but at the same time you need to make your point and ensure that poor behavior isn't repeated.

Here are eight ways to reduce the sting:

1.   Speak quickly
Most brains can be open-minded only for the first two minutes. After that point, they switch to the analytical mode. If I can get the most important point across in the first two minutes, I avoid the other party's inevitable listening shutdown. Before the scheduled feedback delivery, I also write down important points so I can get through them quickly. Criticism has less of an effect if prolonged. After delivering feedback, I give the other person a moment to think about it and ask questions.

2.   Avoid the sandwich
Awhile ago I learned about a "feedback sandwich" (delicious!) in which one would say something positive, then say something critical, and then say something nice again. This sounds good in theory. However, in practice, the positive pieces sound contrived, and only makes the agony last longer. My recommendation? Get the criticism over and done with in as few words as possible. There will be time for positive feedback when the problem is solved.

3.   Be specific
Be as specific as you can in your critiques. I avoid giving the recipient criticism like, "This could be better," or "Ugh." I find it better to explain what exactly needs to be worked on. Feeling personally attacked or not understanding what exactly the issue is puts people on the defensive. Correction can be especially difficult when working with a defensive attitude.

4.   Offer improvements

The goal of criticism should be to help someone make improvements. While giving specific feedback is a great first step on the way to fixing the problem, we'll still need to figure out how to fix it. I don't just point out the mistakes in their work; I give specific suggestions for improvement. But just as in the paragraph above, I'm specific in my suggestions.

5.   Be cool

Before giving negative feedback I always take a deep breath and check my emotions. This is particularly important if the mistake was huge, or affected you personally. Going in with a hot head may get you short-term fixes, but taking time for a reasonable chat can help find underlying issues and even better fixes.

6.   Externalize the criticism

Keep the recipient of criticism as separate as you can from his or her mistake. Criticize the actions, and not the person. Criticizing just the specific activity makes my feedback much less hurtful and much more effective. Just because I may have made a mistake, I am not an idiot.

7.   Frame feedback as growth

My favorite method for delivering negative feedback is to frame the feedback as growth. Asking the question, "See yourself five years from now in your career. Have you advanced? Do you have better skills than you do now?" Most everyone wants to experience career growth. Most everyone wants to feel important. Framing feedback as growth can put the positive spin on criticism so that it doesn't feel like pandering.

8.   Use the magic question

When I'm giving negative feedback for what I perceive to be a major character problem, I use the magic question. "Are you aware...?" This question can help cover the worst offenses.

"Are you aware that people are perceiving you as harsh when you yell?"

"Are you aware that could be received as irritating?"

"Are you aware that the dress you're wearing isn't promoting a polished image?"

(An alternative that reporters sometimes use: "How do you respond to those who say you...?")

By asking the magic question, I allow the recipient of the criticism a way out. And then it's a team effort, figuring out how to move forward.

As a manager, it's tough to give feedback. Many don't bother in an effort to be popular—but offering honest feedback can make your team stronger. Use these tips to help make the feedback easier to give.

Reprinted by permission from American Express Open Forum

7

E-mail, Social Media, and Those Difficult Talks

Sometimes a movie says it all. When it comes to the challenges of social media and difficult talks, the movie is the 2009 George Clooney comedy-drama *Up in the Air*.

The job of Clooney's character, Ryan Bingham, is to fire people from their jobs. Difficult talks are his way of life. Natalie Keener (played by Anna Kendrick), a 20-something techno-arrogant overachiever, recommends that the company cut costs by conducting the "firings" via remote computer access. Why, IBM and Coke have been doing it for years, says the enthusiastic boss.

Ryan believes that Natalie does not fully understand the nature of tough talks involving terminations and, as such, their boss suggests that she accompany Ryan on a business trip. Determined to show the naive girl the error of her logic, Ryan takes her on one of his cross-country firing expeditions, and she starts to realize the disheartening realities of tough talks.

After one series of firings they go to the hotel bar and Natalie shows Ryan a text message from Brian, her fiancée: "I think we should C other people."

Natalie can't believe Brian dumped her via text. "I know, that's like firing people over the Internet or something," says Ryan.

The moral I took away from the film: difficult talks and social media generally don't mix. Yet I see it happening more and more. In one PR office I visited, instead of working out their differences, two PR pros who work in close proximity just chose to un-friend each other on Facebook.

E-mail Is No Place for Those Difficult Talks

Recently, I found myself embroiled in a battle of e-mails... which was ironic in that I give workshops on the topic of difficult talks and was writing this book on the subject. I am regularly on my soapbox on the importance of confronting issues head on. Hypocrite, you say?

Truth be told, sometimes we are most attracted to the topics that we need to learn by teaching. In fact, I've written about difficult talks for years.

So I started to ask myself, "When is it okay to have a tough talk by e-mail?" (Or rather, since an e-mail is not a talk, the question really is "What topics can be addressed via e-mail?") You can substitute texting for e-mail, if you'd like.

Outside of simply the practical limitations of e-mail (e.g. sometimes facts, issues, and concerns are too complex, too multi-various, and "need to have in-the-moment discussion and debate" to be adequately addressed), ask yourself the following tough questions:

1. Are you in any way dehumanizing each other during this process (either through the correspondence or in your own mind)?

2. Are you seeing the other person as anything less than a reasonable, rational, and decent person, with a complex life and feelings, just like your own?

3. Are you copping out or trying to take a shortcut by not engaging the other individual in a face-to-face conversation?

If so, then you need to immediately humanize this person in your eyes. Get on the phone, hear his or her voice and acknowledge the human factor.

So, ask yourself: "What is the topic that you should be addressing live—by phone or in person—which you may be avoiding by using e-mail?"

What might be the benefit of addressing the issue head-on?

Social media are beneficial tools for a lot of things, but not for a difficult talk. E-mail as a supplement to an in-person conversation, however, is often acceptable and even desirable.

In fact, according to David C. Baker, a PR consultant mentioned earlier, because e-mail "communicates very clearly in a directed way," it can dispel the anger and emotion-clouded thought processes the face-to-face conversation may have engendered.

So it's usually beneficial. But, even if it isn't, the consultant comments, there are times when it's necessary, when something needs to be documented or when the remote location of employees makes face-to-face communication difficult.

Quick Tip File: Difficult Conversations at Work
Here is the view of best-selling author Seth Godin, from his blog (http://sethgodin.typepad.com):

"When the outcome of a conversation is in doubt, don't do it by e-mail. And show up in person if you can. The synchronicity of face-to-face conversation gives you the chance to change your tone in midstream. Ask questions. A great question is usually better than a good answer. And don't forget—the value of a long pause is difficult to overstate."

Six Ways to Avoid E-mail Disasters

Here are some great thoughts and tips from Gil Rudawsky, a former reporter and editor. He heads up the crisis communication and issues management practice at GroundFloor Media in Denver. You can read his blog (http://crisis.groundfloormedia.com) or contact him at grudawsky@groundfloormedia.com.

"Let's start with the obvious," says Rudawsky. "Assume that everything you write can be broadcast to the world. Even before blogs and Facebook, this has been the case."

When Rudawsky was a cub reporter, an elderly homeowner sent him a letter she received from her neighbor, who happened to be an attorney. She was involved in a property dispute with him, and this letter threatened the woman with endless legal action that would haunt her every waking (and sleeping) moment.

"I persuaded my editor to print the letter as part of a story on the case," says Rudawsky. "The fallout was amazing. The community rallied in support of the elderly homeowner, and the attorney was inundated with hate mail. He apologized and dropped the suit, and undoubtedly lost a ton of business—and sleep."

Nowadays, the homeowner wouldn't even need to persuade a reporter to do a story; she could just post it to Facebook and let everyone's outrage do the rest, says Rudawsky.

Here are some tips from Rudawsky that can save you from being the (unflattering) talk of the Internet:

1. **"Reply All" pitfalls**. Yes, we've all done it and have had it done to us. Take an extra 10 seconds before you hit "send" and make sure

it's going to the intended parties. I once had a prospective client hit "reply all" to an e-mail I sent him outlining my proposal when he intended to respond only to his partner. He said that he wanted to see my upcoming presentation so he could use my ideas himself. Instead of making him aware of the error, I simply canceled the new business presentation.

2. Auto-fill pitfall. Microsoft Outlook is notorious for auto-filling in the wrong names. Double-check that you are sending to the right person.

3. No poison pen. For whatever reason, nuance is often lost in e-mails. Something you think is funny can be interpreted as offensive. Unless you are corresponding with someone you can trust completely, keep e-mails to the point and devoid of emotion.

4. No downward spiral. With 20 years in a newsroom, I've been called every name in the book. Somewhere along the way, I learned to turn the other cheek. Engaging in useless back and forth with someone who has a different viewpoint doesn't win you any points.

5. Stop, look, and listen. Before you hit "send" on a nasty e-mail, step away from your computer for 30 minutes. By the time you come back, it's likely your blood will have stopped boiling, and you'll delete the missive.

6. Get a buddy. Have a friend or co-worker read your e-mail response before you send it. He or she might offer a more clear-headed point of view and may talk some sense into you. Plus, sometimes it just feels better to have someone other than the intended recipient read your snarky response.

Summing It Up

At work or away, difficult talks are often vital. Yet, many of us try to avoid having them—primarily because they are, indeed, tough.

For reasons legitimate and otherwise, we try to delay having them or seek to sidestep them altogether. We may dislike confrontation, or fear hurting the other's feelings, or agonize about possibly poisoning a relationship. Maybe it is all of these issues.

But those difficult conversations can reap huge rewards, and the sooner you initiate them, the better. With sensitivity, compassion, and regard to the other person's point of view—and adoption of some of the principles outlined in this book—you may find that the talk is not as tough as you imagined, and a positive outcome is possible for all concerned. Please do it!

Appendix

The Straight Line Approach

Sometimes the most effective approach is the most direct.

In those instances where a person's behavior has had an adverse impact on performance and an immediate correction is required, a direct, factual, and unemotional approach can work wonders. If you have any doubts, check out Brad Pitt's performance in *Moneyball*. How his character masters the art of straight talk is powerful stuff!

Try this:

Calm: Get calm and centered.

Private: Ask for a private conversation.

Situation: Describe the situation and its impact on You/The Team/The Business/Other Stakeholders.

Behavior: Explain the behavior you have observed, avoid blame or judgments.

Pause: Pause whenever appropriate to respect the other person's desire to respond.

Preferred Positive: Agree on a preferred behavior and end on a positive note.

Consequences: Only use this if you feel that no true reconciliation and commitment has been reached, and you have reason to believe the behavior may recur. Even then, do not use this as a threat. Use it, rather, as a helpful way of pointing out how the person's failure to change their behavior will affect them. Help them make a choice about their behavior, which will help them.

Adapted with permission from materials by Gary Dichtenberg, President of Professional Development Associates.

Talking the Talk Away from Work

Away from the office, in "real life," we all experience situations that just about cry out for difficult talks, but we often choose to avoid them—at our own peril.

Some examples:

Your spouse, significant other, child or parent, has an annoying habit that fairly drives you up the proverbial wall.

What are your options?

A. Live with it

B. Show your displeasure by scowling, or leaving the room, or screaming "stop it!" every time it happens

C. Send a note, explaining your displeasure

D. Have a candid though difficult conversation about it with the offending party

If you choose D, the likely result can be:

1. The other party never realized that what he or she was doing bothered you so much, and promises to avoid doing it in the future.

2. The other party is angered by your comments and unloads a barrage of criticism about all the things you do that bothers him or her.

3. Your comments are so hurtful, the relationship is threatened.

Which option do you choose? And how do you apply the principles outlined in this book?

Your next-door neighbors have been cordial and helpful to you for years—digging your car out after a snowstorm, giving you

vegetables from their garden, inviting you to their parties. But their son plays music so loud, you can't sleep.

What are your options?

    A. Live with it

    B. Get a petition going on Facebook

    C. Send a note explaining your gripe

    D. Invite the parents for a heart-to-heart talk

If you choose D, the likely result can be:

    1. He plays the music louder

    2. His parents stop talking to you

    3. He promises to turn down the volume, or maybe not play at such volume after 9 p.m.

Which option do you choose?

The family across the street is also very nice, even driving you or your spouse to the doctor's office when you were incapacitated. But the husband is given to expressing vulgar, anti-ethnic opinions.

What are your options?

    A. Live with it

    B. Make vulgar references to his ethnic group

    C. Send him a note describing your displeasure

    D. Ask him for a one-on-one chat about his offensive habit

If you choose D, the likely result can be:

1. A nasty comment about your ethnic group

2. He starts a whispering campaign about you

3. He explains it's just his style, he means nothing by it, and promises to try muzzle his outbursts

And finally, a dear relative or friend, who has been close to you and your family for years, will not be invited to a big celebration in your family due to limitations on the number of invitees. This person is overly sensitive, easily hurt, and will not accept a logical explanation.

What are your options?

A.   Hope she doesn't learn about the celebration (most unlikely)

B. Pray she'll be out of the country on the date of the event

C. Simply gear yourself for a long-lasting "mad" on her part

D. Send a note with reasons she's not being invited

E. Invite her for tea, and plan to broach the painful subject, as difficult as that is likely to be

If you choose E, the likely result can be:

1. The hurt party breaks all ties with you and your family

2. You're never invited to any event sponsored by her

3. She understands perfectly, appreciates the fact you chose to explain the situation to her, and your relationship is stronger than ever

No result is assured in any of these situations, but by your following ideal "difficult talk" principles, the chances of the optimum outcome are tremendously enhanced.

Which Difficult Talks Are You Avoiding?

NOW, CALULATE THE COST TO YOU AND YOUR ORGANIZATION

It's possible there are some who take delight in confrontation, but the fact is that most of us rank unpleasant workplace discussion a few rungs below Shark Attack on the universal ladder of enjoyment.

Unfortunately, difficult talks are a fact of business life. And here's another fact: they don't always go smoothly or even as planned. People are emotional beings and sometimes they just don't want to "hear it."

The good news is that there are basic strategies that can help make confrontations, verbal skirmishes, and angry exchanges far more manageable.

Alan Cohen's Those Difficult Talks for PR Pros(SM) workshops, seminars, and lectures will help to take the angst and anxiety out of office confrontations and help you keep your sanity in the process.

We'll show you how to take other people's emotions and vulnerabilities into account and how to use them to make a bumpy road smoother. You'll learn the power of framing–how omitting extraneous details can make bad news easier to swallow. We'll show you how to recognize when it's not you, those moments when your conversational counterpart isn't responding to you but to other factors in his or her life.

And we'll demonstrate how confronting difficulty head-on– thoughtfully and sympathetically but without ego or emotion–can earn you the respect and admiration not only of the other person in the room, but of everyone else in the office.

Our workshop addresses a topic that many would rather avoid. And while our workshop might not leave you relishing your next charged confrontation, it will leave you much better equipped to not only handle it, but benefit and grow from it as well.

Alan offers additional workshops including Effective Communications, Leadership Theory and Skills, and Brainstorming Techniques.

Workshops can also be customized.

For more information, visit: www.actsofbalance.com and make sure to go to the bonus section for additional resources.

Working With Alan Cohen

Alan Cohen offers business programs to help companies increase productivity and well-being. As executive coach, trainer, brainstorm facilitator and speaker, Alan helps organizations better navigate their ever-changing business landscape and thus achieve greater success, fulfillment, and balance.

He works with executives, teams and small business owners, to become more meaningfully engaged and communicate more effectively, resulting in greater performance and highly improved business results.

If you are interested in learning more about hosting a Those Difficult Talks for PR Pros (SM) seminar, or other training programs or keynotes offered by Alan Cohen, contact information is as follows:

Alan Cohen
Alancohen@actsofbalance.com
(212) 219-1544
(646) 489-4989

Corporate Website: www.actsofbalance.com

For additional Those Difficult Talks for PR Pros™ resources, including worksheets and videos, visit www.actsofbalance.com, or e-mail: alancohen@actsofbalance.com.

To order copies of *Those Difficult Talks for PR Pros™* in quantity, please contact Alan Cohen directly at alancohen@actsofbalance.com.

Bonus Materials Offer

Thanks for buying my book.

As a special thank you for your

purchase, please access special

bonus material at

www.actsofbalance.com

Acknowledgments

Writing a book is no easy feat. Having a village of people to help, coach, support and believe in you makes all the difference in the world. I am blessed to have an awesome support team.

Hopefully, the following list won't leave out anyone important, sparing me from having any of "Those Difficult Talks" with those I may have inadvertently neglected.

Drumroll please:

Scott Slavin, who helped me design the checklists, and worked closely to develop the workshop from which this book emanates.

The book itself: Henry DeVries, for his coaching; my Dad, Joel, for his editing; Jorge Noranjo, for cover design, and Benoit Cortet, for the book cover photo; Richard Dedor, for his help with social media to get the word out. My appreciation goes to Eric Taylor for teaching me how to market and sell, and for his incredible energy for this project.

Thank you to all of the experts quoted in the book and those who provided wonderful testimonials.

Keith Sherman, who encouraged me to write the book.

Janet Tyler at Airfol for writing the foreword, and her staff, for being so open to the Those Difficult Tasks for PR Pros™ model.

Thank you to my great clients and coach friends, including my pals at Idea Champions, iPEC Coaching, and Roving Coach, who inspire me every day.

To my family—Ann, Ivan, Harvey, Ali, Paula, Mom, and Dad (so great I have mentioned twice)

And last but not least, my partner, Barry Rosenthal, for all of his support, advice, and believing in me.

About the Author

Alan Cohen, MBA, Professional Certified Coach (PCC), has more than 25 years of business experience in the areas of public relations, marketing, human resources, leadership training, and development. As executive coach, trainer, brainstorm facilitator, and speaker, Alan serves professionals in public relations, marketing, and the media, as well as other industries, to help them better navigate their ever-changing business landscape and thus achieve greater success, fulfillment, and balance.

Through his coaching, he helps executives and small-business owners become more meaningfully engaged and communicate more effectively, resulting in leading their organizations to greater performance and highly improved business results.

An active member of PRSA's Counselors Academy, Alan has worked with such major PR agencies as Airfoil Public Relations, Text 100, Peppercom, Kaplow Communications, Maloney & Fox (a Wagner Edstrom company), Strategic Objectives, Start-Thinking, Clairemont Communications and FerenComm, and with PR executives at Edelman, Dan Klores, PMK, Fleishman Hillard, Ketchum, and Morris-King.

Prior to starting his own coaching business, Alan served as the Director of Communications for The Broadway League, the national trade association for the commercial theatre industry, presenter of the Tony Awards. As Communications Director, his most notable contribution was leading the crisis communications team during the Broadway stagehands strike.

Prior to his position with the Broadway League, he served as Director of Corporate Training and Development for Scholastic, where he established and supervised the company's management training curriculum. At Scholastic, he was also Director of Publicity and led the publicity team promoting the acclaimed *Harry Potter* book series. As Vice President at Serino Coyne and Rogers and Cowan public relations, Alan supervised public relations and cultural sponsorship activities. At Robinson Lehrer Montgomery, also as Vice President, he led consumer publicity campaigns for United Airlines, AOL's "Find A Job" service and AOL's Small Business and Life

Management programs.

Alan holds a bachelor's degree in English and Theatre from Connecticut College, and an MBA from Fordham University's Graduate School of Business, where his focus was leadership development. He is an accredited member of the International Coach Federation (ICF) and is one of only 2,000 Professional Certified Coaches in the world.

He is also a trainer for The Institute for Professional Excellence in Coaching, one of the only International Coach Federation (ICF) accredited coaching institutes in the world, and a trained brainstorm facilitator through Idea Champions. For IPEC, he teaches coaching skills to coaches seeking ICF accreditation, entrepreneurs, and leaders.

He is certified in the Energy Leadership Assessment Tool (www.energyleadership.com), which helps the professional develop a personally effective leadership style that positively influences and changes not only the individual, but also colleagues and the organization as a whole.

Alan has been a guest speaker at PRSA's Counselors Academy, the Fashion Institute of Technology, Fordham Graduate School of Business, Rutgers University, mediabistro, the Commercial Theater Institute, and Pinnacle Worldwide.